Piano Time Jazz Duets

Book 1

Pauline Hall

MUSIC DEPARTMENT

OXFORD
UNIVERSITY PRESS

OXFORD

UNIVERSITY PRESS

Great Clarendon Street, Oxford OX2 6DP, England
198 Madison Avenue, New York, NY 10016 USA

Oxford University Press is a department of the University of Oxford.
It furthers the University's aim of excellence in research, scholarship,
and education by publishing worldwide

First published 2006

16

ISBN 0-19-335597-3 978-0-19-335597-2

Illustrations by Andy Hammond

Music and text origination by
Barnes Music Engraving Ltd., East Sussex ·
Printed in Great Britain on acid-free paper by
Halstan & Co. Ltd., Amersham, Bucks.

Contents

Takin' it easy

Stephen Duro

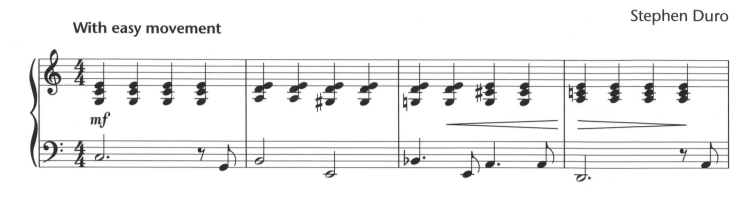

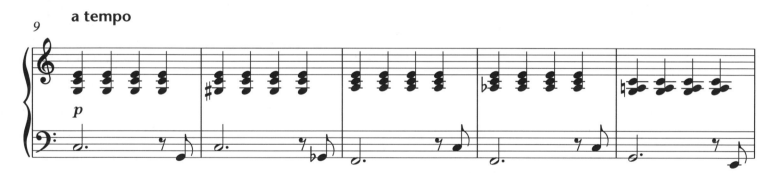

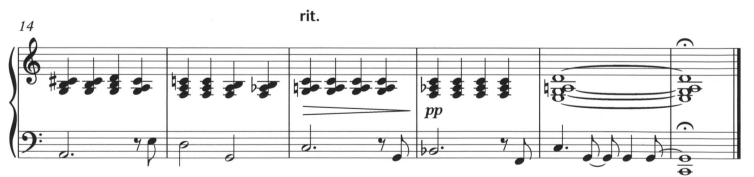

Takin' it easy

With easy movement
Play RH an octave higher

Stephen Duro

poco rit.

a tempo

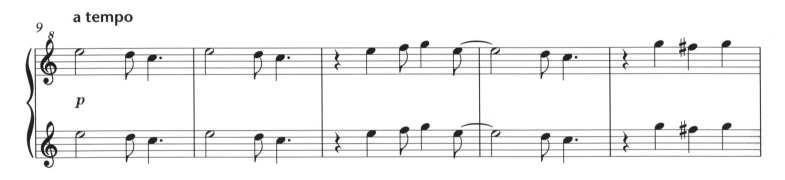

rit.

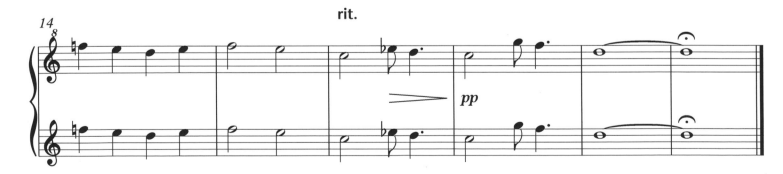

Can't stop the beat

David Blackwell

Happily

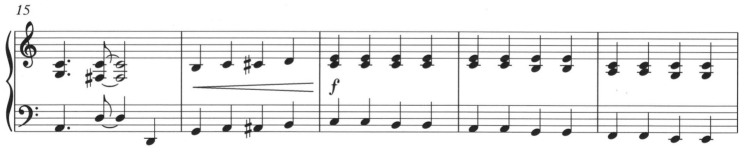

Can't stop the beat

Happily

David Blackwell

Can't stop the beat,   can't stop the beat,   can't stop the rhy-thm   in my feet!

Busybody bossa

Paul Drayton

Steady bossa nova

Busybody bossa

Paul Drayton

Steady bossa nova
Play RH an octave higher

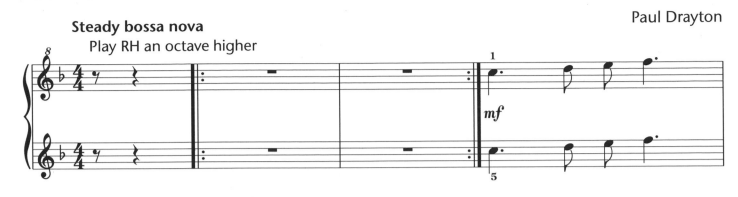

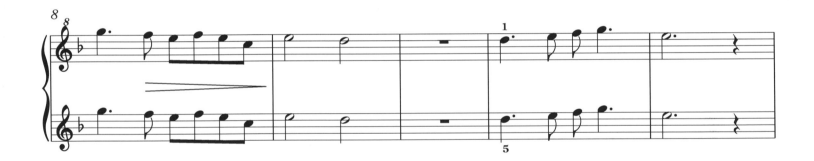

Big Feet

Alan Bullard

12

left right left right, walk-ing down the street, Big Feet, so neat!

Caramba!

Fiona Macardle

Lively and rhythmic

Primo

Lively and rhythmic

Secondo

5

Afternoon stroll

Stephen Duro

Afternoon stroll

Light swing (♫ = ♩♪)

Play RH an octave higher

Stephen Duro

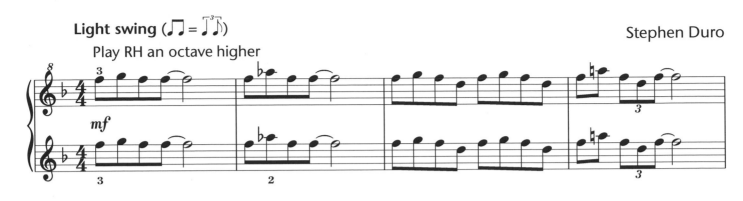

Secondo

Coconut rumba

Roy Stratford

Steady and rhythmic

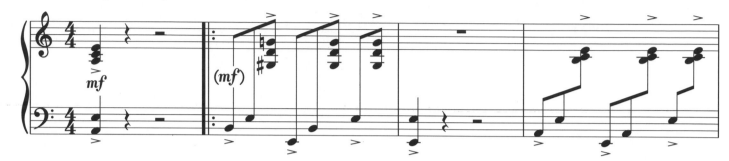

16

Coconut rumba
Steady and rhythmic
Play RH an octave higher

Roy Stratford

Lollipop rock

Pauline Hall

Lollipop rock

Pauline Hall

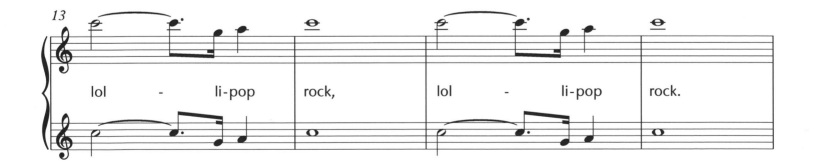

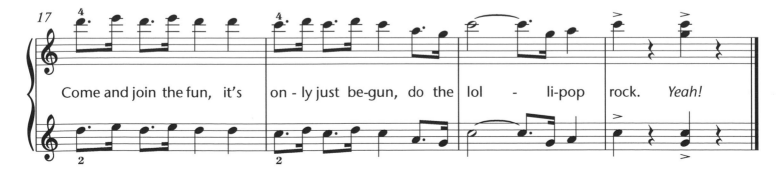

Follow a groove

Here's a chance for you to make up your own duet.

Primo   Right hand either copies the left hand an octave higher, or improvises using the same hand position. Try starting the right-hand phrases on different beats of the bar. Listen out! Some notes will fit better than others.

Alan Bullard

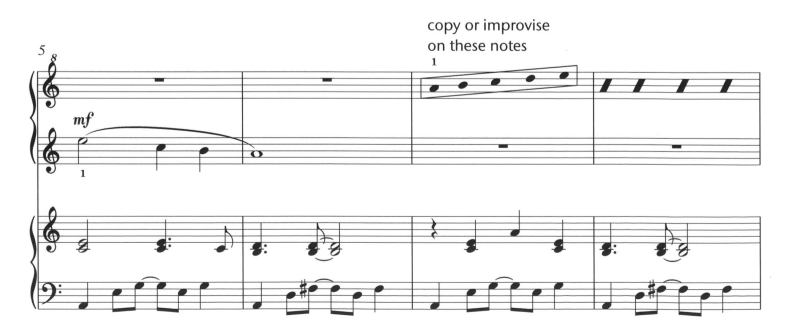

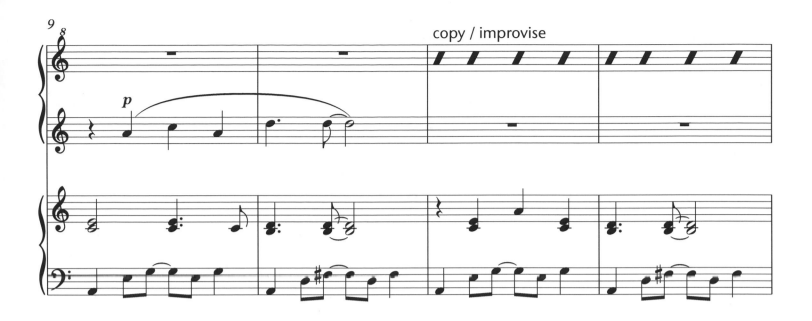

copy / improvise

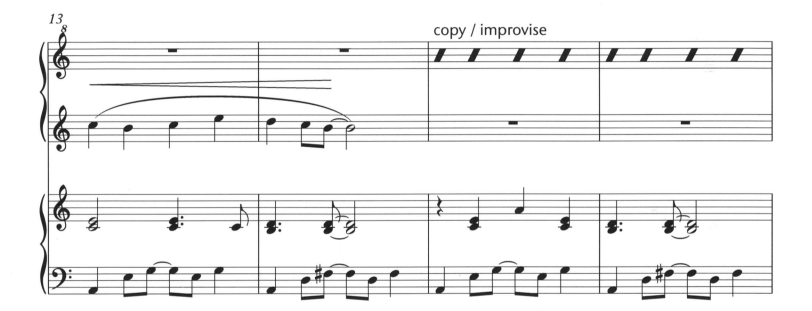

copy / improvise

(decorate the final chord!)

copy / improvise

Boogie baby

Stephen Duro

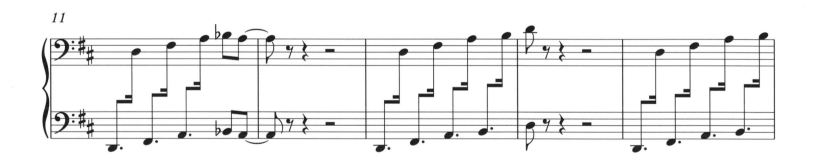

Boogie baby

Stephen Duro

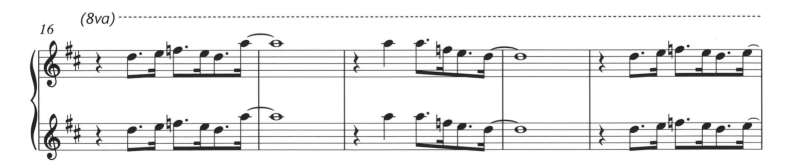

Faraway

Alan Bullard

24

Faraway

Alan Bullard

Algy and the bear

Pauline Hall

With menace (swing)

Algy and the bear

Pauline Hall

Café tango

Fiona Macardle

A bit like Bill

Charles Beale

A bit like Bill

Charles Beale

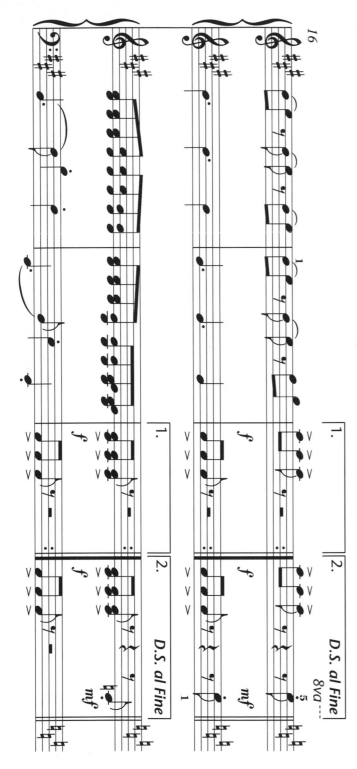

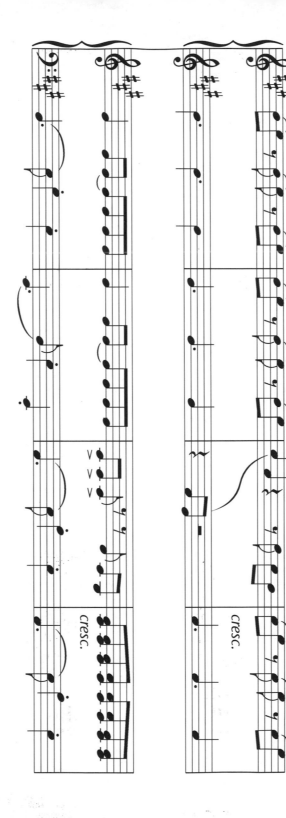

A bit like Bill

Charles Beale

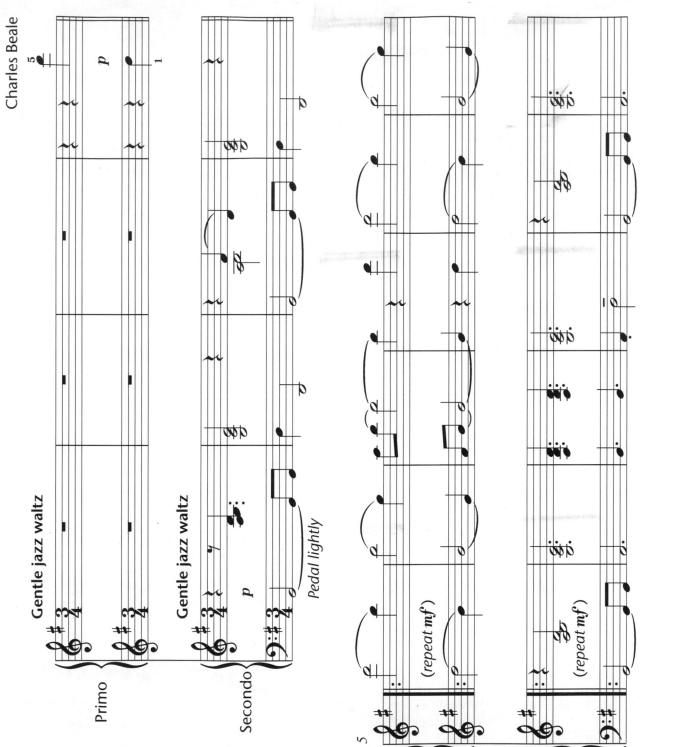
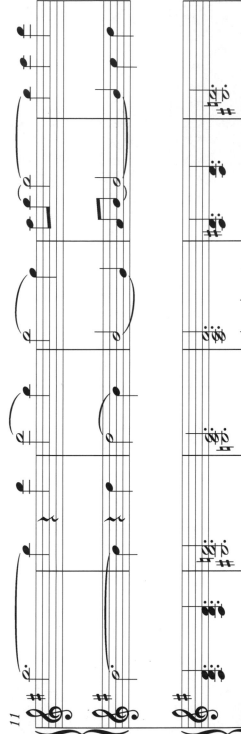

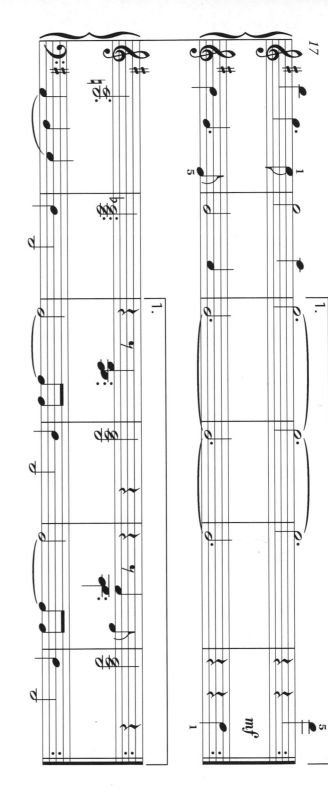
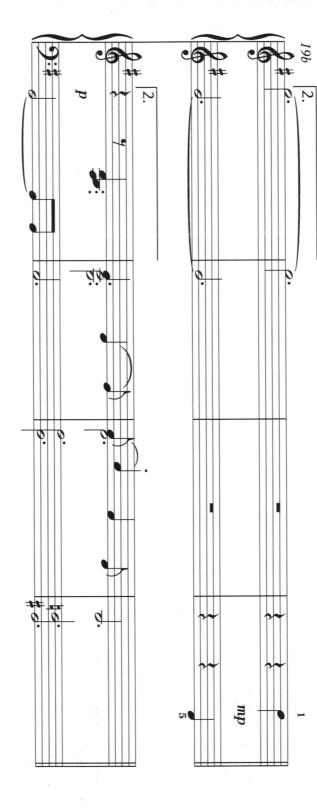
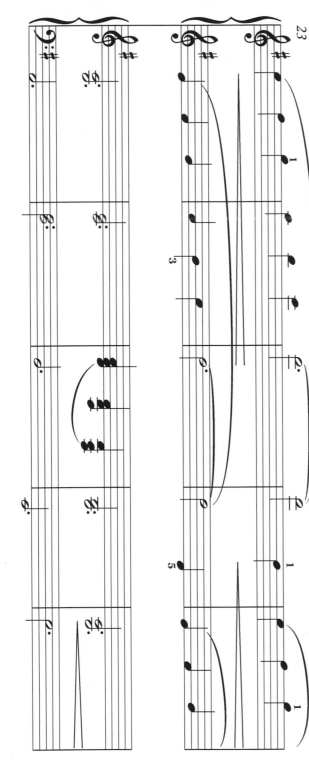

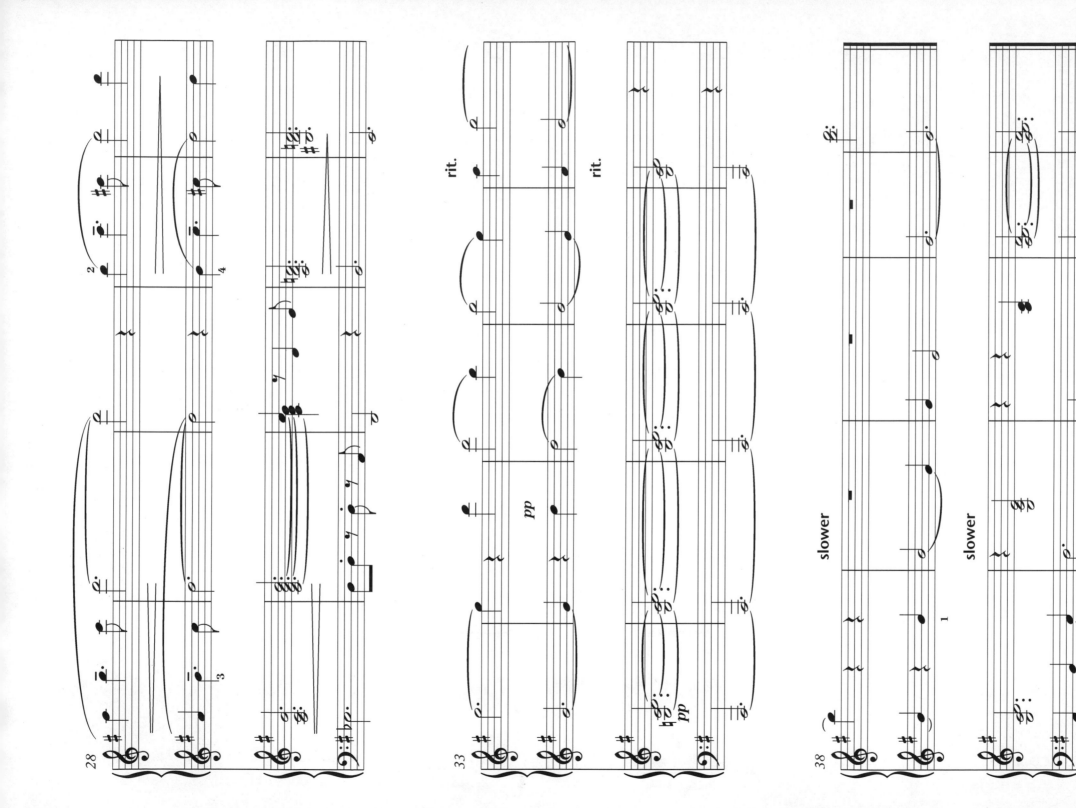